Circle the picture that begins with **C**. **C**ow

Trace the mitten to make **2** mittens.

Color the mitten.

Circle ○ the **sense** you use.

Color all the □ **red**.

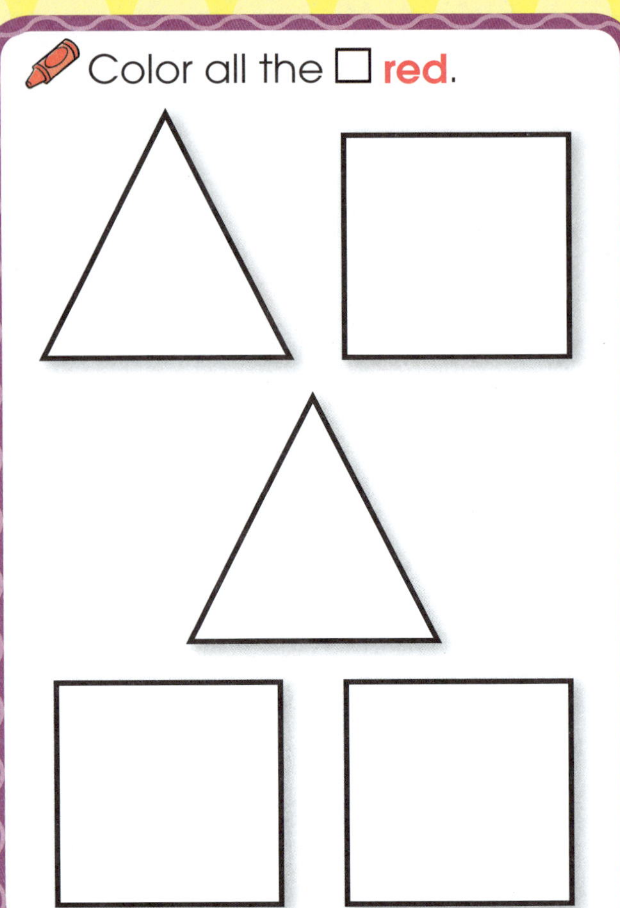

✓ the picture that begins with **E**. **E**gg

Draw a line through all the **Y**'s.

Start

Y	Y	D	W
V	Y	Y	H
V	U	Y	Y
U	V	U	Y
W	X	V	Y

Finish

✓ the light that tells you to STOP.

Circle ◯ the person who helps sick animals.

✓ what is going **up**.

Circle ○ the picture that begins with **A**. Apple

Circle ○ the group that is **1 less than 4**.

✓ the pictures with only **1 of a kind**.

Circle ◯ the **2** pictures that **go together**.

Circle ◯ the picture that begins with **W**. **W**atch

Circle ◯ **1** to show what happened **first**.
Circle ◯ **2** to show what happened **next**.
Circle ◯ **3** to show what happened **last**.

1 2 3

1 2 3

1 2 3

Circle ○ the 🐢 that is **on** the log.

Circle ○ the cupcake that is **different**.

Draw **6** ● on the ladybug.
Color.

✓ **10** 🐛 in the picture.

Color the flower with **8** petals red.

Color to finish the **pattern**.

Color to finish the **pattern**.

Draw a line to where a  lives.

✓ the picture that begins with **H**. **H**amburger

Draw a line to **match** the cookie cutter to its cookie.

✓ the scarecrows that are the **same**.

Circle ○ the group of **3** .

Circle ○ the picture that begins with **N**. **N**est

 Color the picture.

1 = red 2 = green 3 = blue

✓ the picture that begins with **J.** Jet

✗ the picture that does **not belong**.

Circle ◯ **1** to show what happened **first**.
Circle ◯ **2** to show what happened **next**.
Circle ◯ **3** to show what happened **last**.

1 2 3 1 2 3 1 2 3

Circle the picture that begins with **B.** Bee

the animal that **weighs** the most.

Color the shape that is **different**.

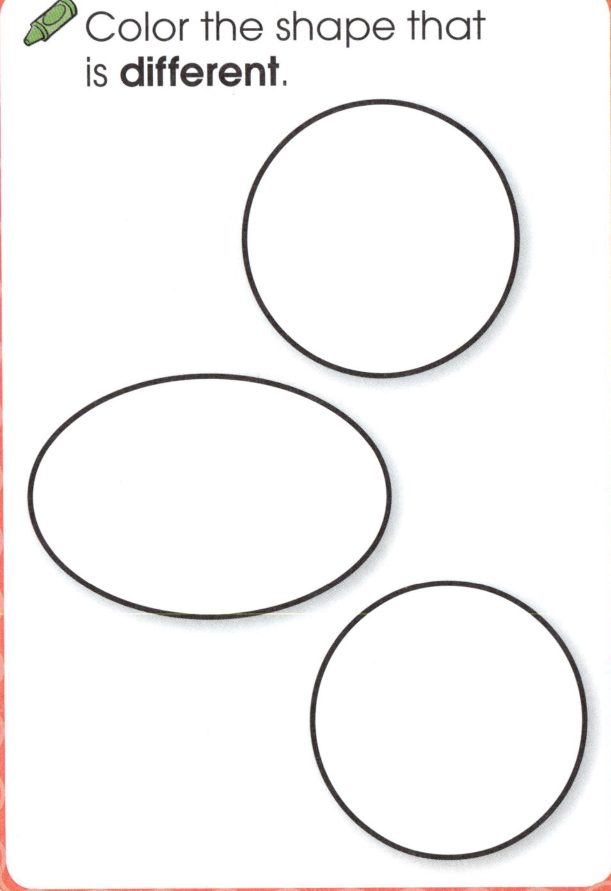

Draw a line through all the **Q**'s.

Start

Q	Q	Q	O
O	Y	Q	D
Q	Q	Q	P
Q	C	O	G
Q	Q	Q	Q

Finish

Color **1** more lollipop.

Circle how **many** there are now.

1 2 3

$2 + 1 =$ ____

Count and color **5** beach balls.

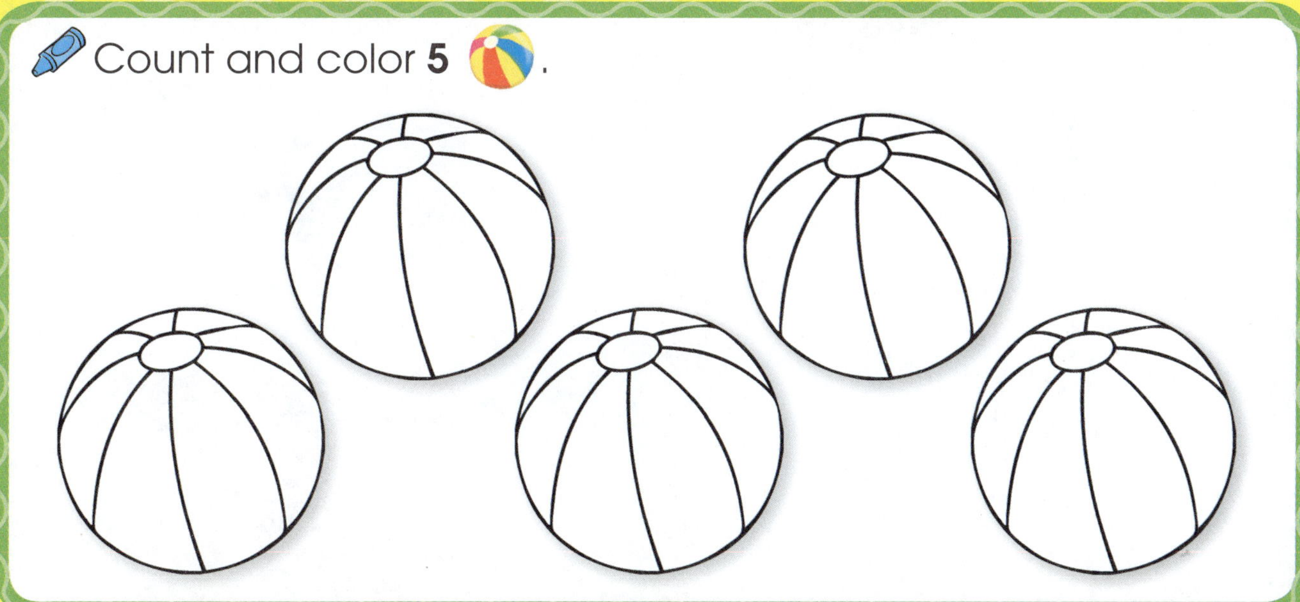

Circle the person who helps you when you are sick.

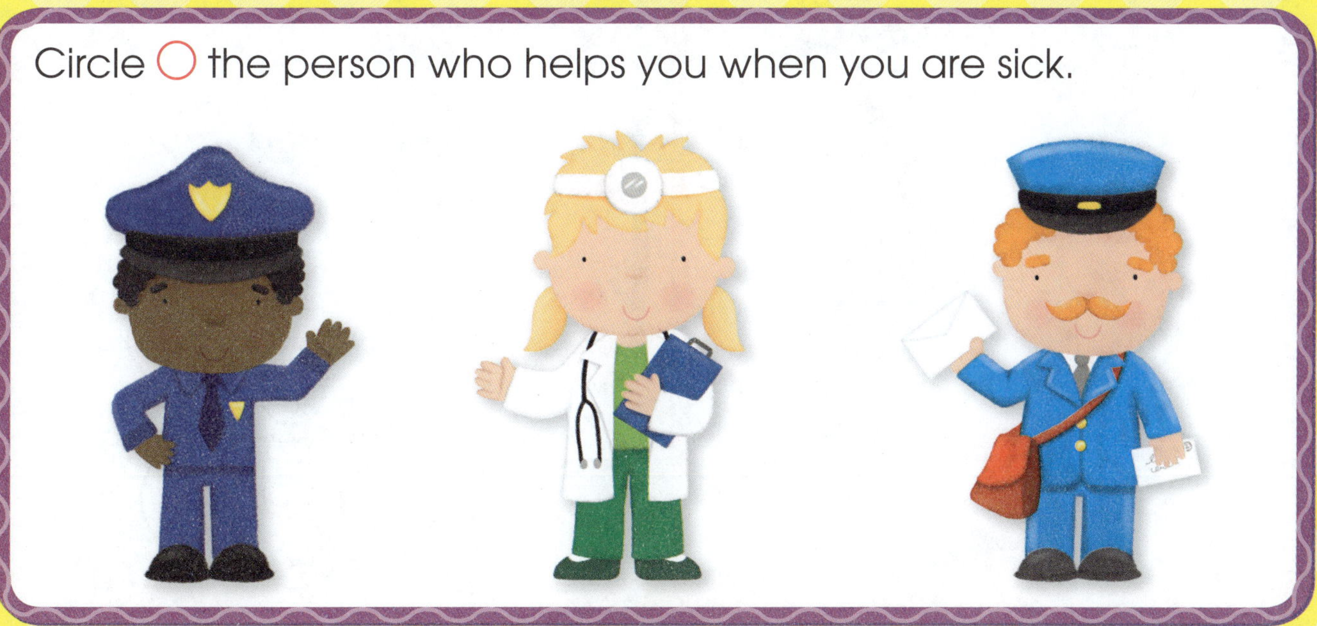

Circle the picture that **rhymes** with .

Circle the picture that begins with **S**.  **S**un

Color to finish the **pattern**.

Circle ◯ the **2** pictures that **rhyme**.

✓ the picture that begins with **G**. **G**love

Draw a line between the that **match**.

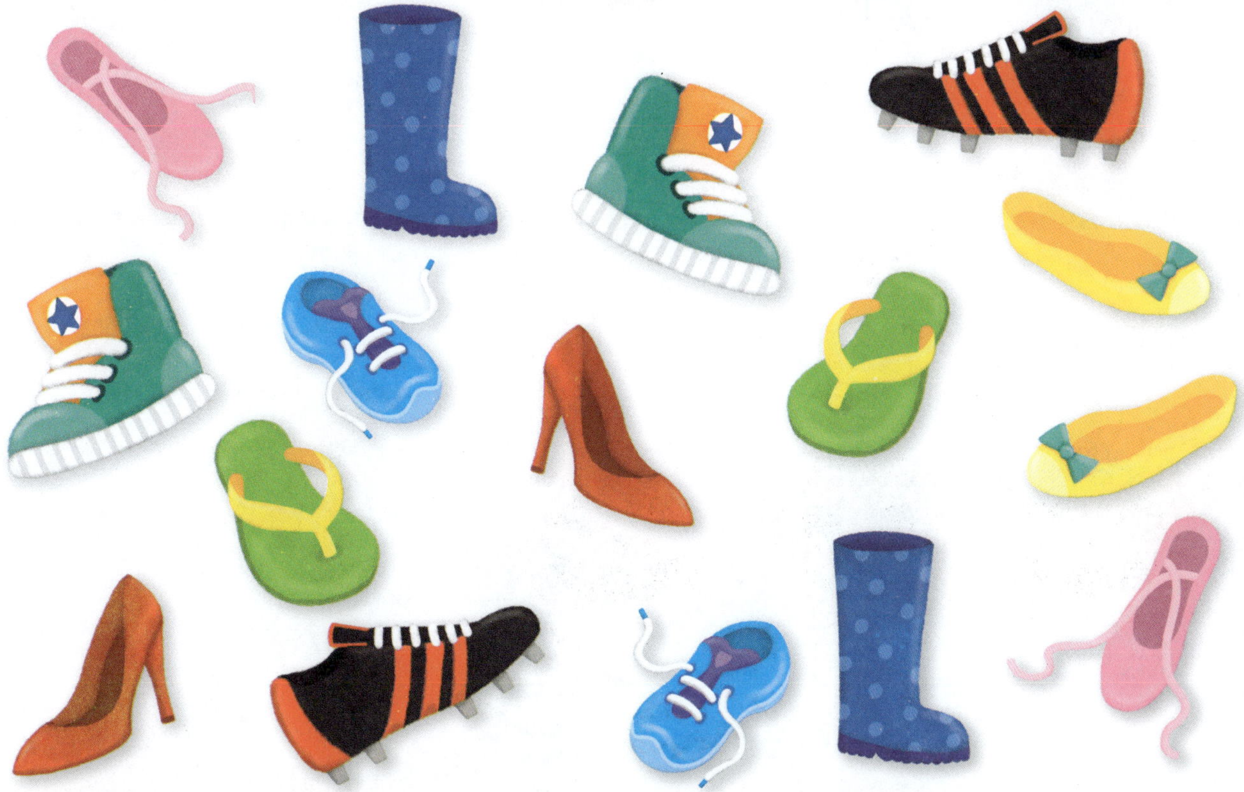

✓ 9  in the picture.

Circle ◯ the person who is pointing **right**.

Circle ◯ the **2** words that are the **same**.

see

cat

saw

see

 Color **1** more .

Circle ◯ **how many** there are now.

3 4 5

$3 + 1 =$ ____

5 things **wrong** in the picture.

ZOO

Color the picture that begins with **P**. **P**ie

Count and color **7** .

Circle ◯ the person who is **sad**.

Circle ◯ the picture that begins with **U**. **U**p

Color to finish the **pattern**.

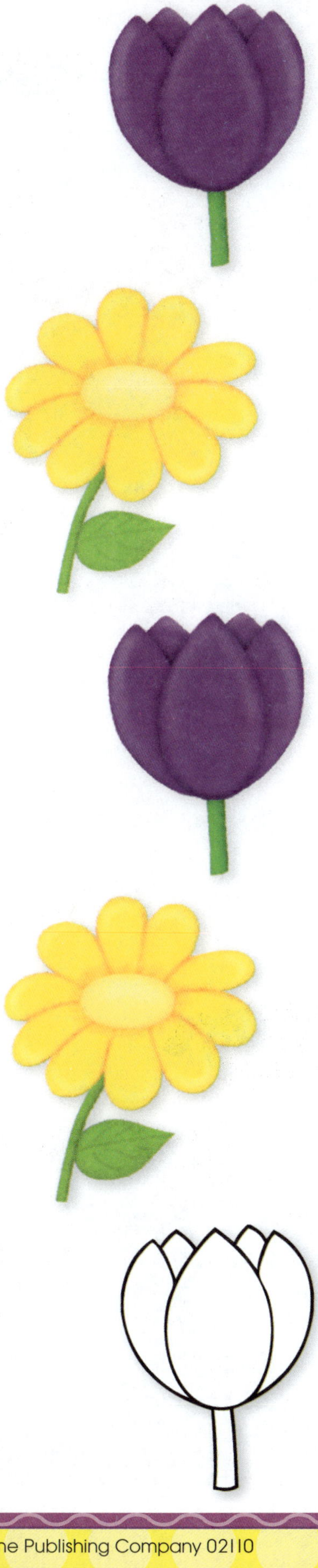

Draw a line through all the **Z**'s.

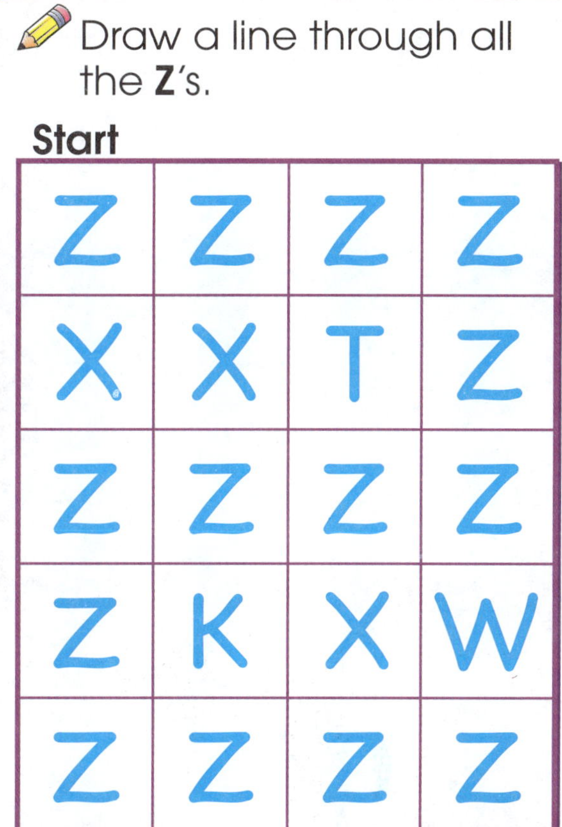

✓ the picture that begins with I. ink Ink

Find and circle ◯ the hidden pictures.

Circle ◯ the picture that begins with **D**. **D**oll

✗ what does **not belong**.

Circle ◯ the group of **12**.

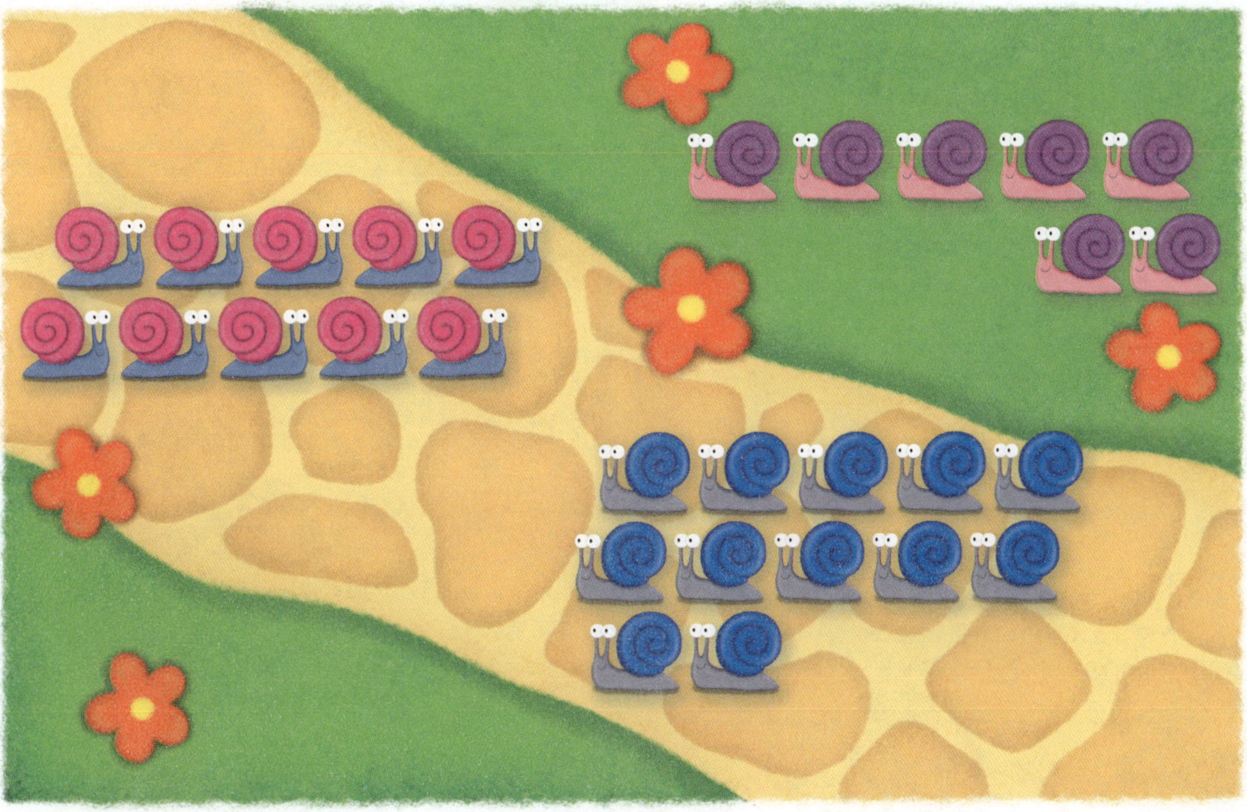

Circle ○ the picture that begins with **M**. **M**ouse

✓ what you would wear in the summer.

Circle ○ the number that comes **before**.

___ 3 4 5

2 3 4

___ 5 6 7

3 4 5

Circle ○ the **2** pictures that **go together**.

Count. Color **4** blue.

Circle the girl who is **under** the .

You ate **1** .

Circle how many **are left**.

1 2 3

3 - 1 = ____

Circle ○ the kite that is **down**.

Color to finish the **pattern**.

Circle ○ the picture that begins with **L**. **L**eaf

Circle ◯ the **tall** clown.
✓ the **short** clown.

Circle ◯ the picture that begins with **R**. **R**ainbow

✓ **11** fish in the picture.

Circle ◯ **1** to show what happened **first**.
Circle ◯ **2** to show what happened **next**.
Circle ◯ **3** to show what happened **last**.

1 2 3 1 2 3

1 2 3

Circle ◯ the animal that is **fast**.
✗ the animal that is **slow**.

Circle ◯ the number that comes **after 7**.

8 11 7

Circle ◯ the number that comes **after 9**.

5 7 10

Two eggs are hatching in the nest.
Circle ◯ how many **are left**.

1 2 3

3 - 2 = ____

 Draw a line through all the **X**'s.

Start

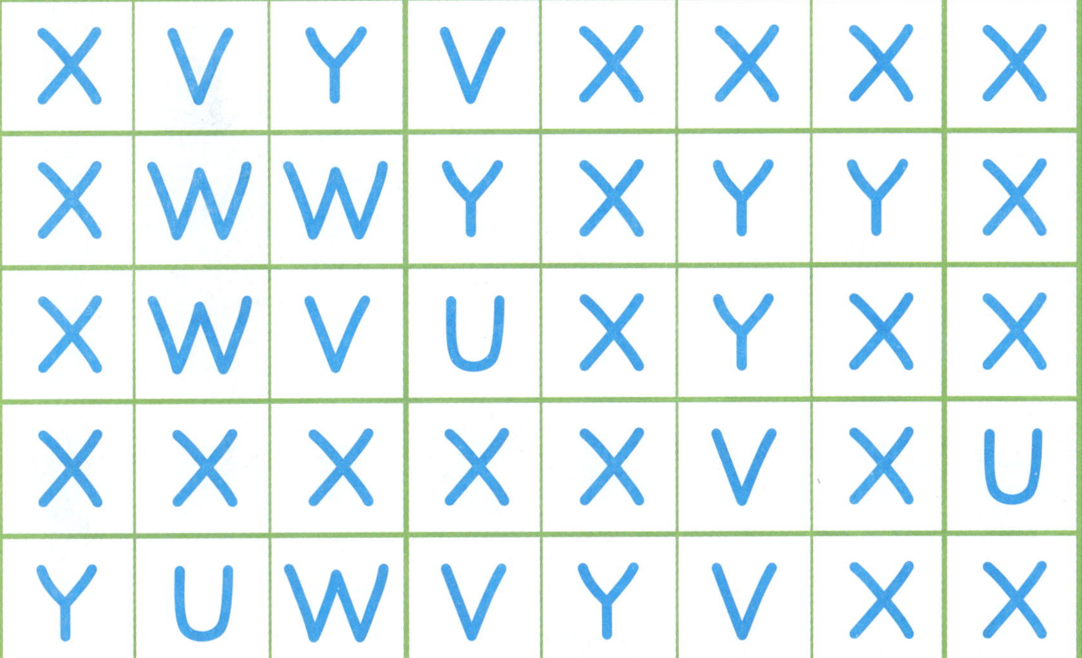

X	V	Y	V	X	X	X	X
X	W	W	Y	X	Y	Y	X
X	W	V	U	X	Y	X	X
X	X	X	X	X	V	X	U
Y	U	W	V	Y	V	X	X

Finish

 Color the picture that begins with **K**.  **K**ey

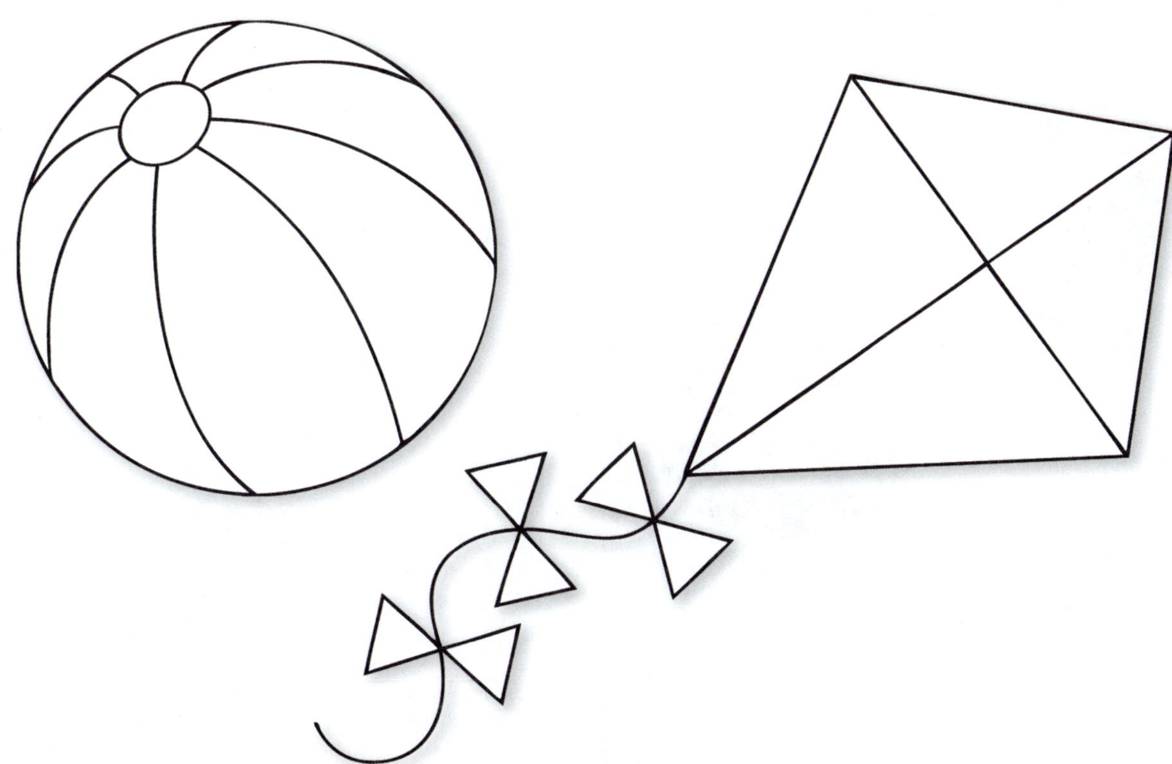

✓ all the △ in the picture.
Circle ○ **how many** there are.

7 8 9

Circle ○ the picture that begins with **F**.  **F**rog

Circle ○ the number that comes **after**.

2 3 4 ___

3 4 5

4 5 6 ___

6 7 8

Trace and color the shape that comes **next**.

Circle the picture that begins with **O**. **O**ctopus

Circle the bee that is **off** the .

Connect the dots from **1** to **12**.
Color the picture.

Circle ○ the picture that begins with **V**. **V**iolin

Circle ○ the group that is **1 more than 3**.

✗ **8** things **wrong** in the picture.

Circle ○ the picture that begins with **T**. **T**urtle

✓ what you would wear in the winter.

Trace the **2** □.
Color.

Circle ○ the animal that lives here.